DANGEROUS WOMAN

Poetry for
the Ageless

To Colleen –

We are all —
fearless + dangerous –
+ Ageless

Frances H Halpern

4/23/18

DANGEROUS WOMAN

Poetry for the Ageless

FRANCES H. KAKUGAWA

WATERMARK
PUBLISHING

ISBN: 978-1-935690-91-7 (print edition)

Library of Congress Control Number: 2017952068

Cover design & artwork by Jason Kimura
Interior design and production by Dawn Sakamoto Paiva
Author's photo by Jason Kimura

Watermark Publishing
1000 Bishop Street, Suite 806
Honolulu, Hawai'i 96813
Telephone (toll-free): 1-866-900-BOOK
Website: www.bookshawaii.net

Printed in the United States of America

Dedicated to Red

OTHER BOOKS BY FRANCES H. KAKUGAWA

FOR CAREGIVERS

Mosaic Moon: Caregiving Through Poetry

Breaking the Silence: A Caregiver's Voice

I Am Somebody:
Bringing Dignity and Compassion to Alzheimer's Caregiving

✸

CHILDREN'S BOOKS

Wordsworth the Poet

Wordsworth Dances the Waltz

Wordsworth! Stop the Bulldozer!

Wordsworth, It's In Your Pocket!

✸

MEMOIRS

Teacher, You Look Like a Horse!
Lessons from the Classroom

Kapoho: Memoir of a Modern Pompeii

✸

POETRY

Sand Grains

White Ginger Blossom

Golden Spike

The Path of Butterflies

Contents

Introduction

It began when I was six years old. My first-grade teacher read a poem about flowers nodding their heads in the sun. It was then that I began my love affair with words and poetry.

The poems in this book were written over a span of sixty years, from my younger days up to the present, where I am—according to statistics—living the last decade of my life. Selected poems from my first four books, published in the '70s, are also included; their relevancy does not seem to have aged along with me.

Organizing this collection chronologically would give a false impression that the things I wrote about were happening in some logical sequence, each poem somehow leading to the next and then the next or building off the previous. The reality is that any of these poems could have been written when I was twenty-one or eighty. The years have not changed my questions about the nature of being, my search for myself as a woman and person, my political awareness or my desire to help create a peaceful and more humane world.

Our passionate desire for answers to life's existential questions, the need to understand our relationship with nature and the world beyond the self, do not diminish with time. Triumphs, conflicts and disappointments; a curiosity about others; introspection about our past and future—I hope all these inform my poetry from youth up to the present moment.

Simply put, age does not identify us, life does. So, whether you're a teen, a forty-something or ninety-nine, I hope there is a poem for you in this book. Enjoy. ✸

— *Frances H. Kakugawa*

Section I

A Poet's Life

I knew at age six that poets were a special group of people who, like magicians, created images in my head with words alone, and I was determined to become one of them. I began with silly rhymes: "Oh see the dancing waves, go crashing through the caves." I kept all my childhood poems in a secret shoe box which was left behind during the evacuation when Kīlauea Volcano sent her fingers of lava over our village. But most of them I knew by heart, so I included a few in my children's books more than fifty years later.

I have lived with my antennae fully extended, knowing there are poems waiting to be written and with octopus-like suckers they just won't let go until I attach words and images to each. If only they came with words—but no, that is the poet's work.

The poems in this section speak of this process of that relentless search for the perfect word(s) to bring into form those images, feelings, ideas and thoughts that cling on until released in some poetic form, and of the gift it brings to poet and readers. ✳

A POET'S LIFE

The Black crow—back again.
His summons—relentless,
demanding, shrill.

From the garden—beckons
the rose bush slow dancing
breathe-in fragrance.

Delicate latticed leaf designs
by rose bugs—our petal face
Wet in dewdrop.

Morning glories, too, purplish blue
on Cerulean sky, sprinkled shy pink blush
on chicken wire fence.

If only I had her brushes—
To draw me into the purple
Sleep. The final

overhead, sunflowers
with freckled face, host summer feasts.
At my feet—weeds

suffocate petunias and pansies.
I bend to pull them out, weeds.
The flap of crow wings stuns.

Over the fence, a straight blade of grass
stands tall as a solitary soldier—
roots in a sidewalk crack.

The Crow atop the Cypress tree
will not go away. Will not go away.
Until I put pen to paper. ✸

NO, I'M NOT DONE

Undefined, balled and tossed
From second story balconies
Followed by rage, confusion, frustration
And left-over luggage of evicted muse,
The poet cannot leave. ✤

I'M DONE

Before she could take that second sip,
The poem disappears into a cup
Of hot steam.

Her hand over her belly,
The gurgle and grind of a
One-night stand, some what's-his-name lover
Gives her cramps. A voice somewhere says, "Push! Push!"
She bends over, ink flows.
Regurgitated. A Poem. ❀

I want to write that poem for you,
That poem of such magnificence
It would be called a masterpiece.

THE POEM UNWRITTEN

I want to write the poem that says
What poets have tried to convey
Since the beginning of time
On stone-age walls.

I want to write that poem for you
To turn you inside out
With my perfect schema
And metaphor genius,

A poem that would bring
The greats to their knees
And shame the sonnets
Of Shakespeare.

I want to write a poem
That correctly pronounces all my feelings,
The ones never spoken
When I am with you.

Alas. We are the poem
That cannot be written,
It cannot be found
In all of my ink wells.

So this is my poem
Of that poem
That cannot be written. ✸

A POEM SPEAKS

I am poem…
Mender of broken souls…

I file the edges of jagged nails,
Torn and clawed with human toil.

I take the salt from human tears
To wash out human pain.

I flow the blood caked deep
Beneath each punctured wound.

I lift the weary to their feet,
To rinse away the Bittersweet.

Come, my child, and walk my shores…
I am mender of human souls. ✾

A POET'S SANCTUM

Elizabeth Barrett Browning
Had her bedroom.
Emily Dickinson
The lonely attic.
Thoreau, his pond.
Dylan Thomas, his pub.
I, and I
A coffee shop,
My pen
And you. ✸

The dead kept me alive
All those years, growing up
Confined to a village so isolated,
So unpaved, so un-vehicled,

DEAD POETS ALIVE

So battery-run. Our three-party line
A public service gossip center.

The speechless dead took me beyond
Montgomery Ward catalogs, dream-makers
Until one day I discovered an oracle
Within the pages, poets long gone.
Promises of wondrous worlds
For the me not yet formed.

Oh, how I mourn that "breath of ecstasy"
To travel that road where dreams can go
Though not so much "in depth and breadth and height
My soul can reach."
And like a little "nobody" to "lie down
To pleasant dreams."

It was the dead who gave me such dreams
And showed the woman I'd become
To wander where they could not go
And wonder at what got them there.
My morning still lay ahead, I still "had miles to go."
But oh, how "I wandered lonely as a cloud." ✿

OBABAN*

My eighty-year-old grandmother stood
On the sidewalk in Hilo, facing Kress Store.
"I wonder," she said in Japanese, "how
Hilo will look long after I'm gone.
I wish I could stay."

Had I been wiser, I would have said—
"Obaban, what if eighty years ago, your mother
Said this to you, She couldn't stay
So she gave her eyes to you.
Now it's my turn. I will be here.
I'll take pictures, Obaban."

I stand where she once stood
With my broken promises. Kress Store is gone.
Hilo Drugs is gone. There are no photos,
But I wrote these poems.
Just these poems, I wrote them. ❀

*Grandmother

Over the intercom, my name fills the room,
followed by a press release on *Mosaic Moon.*
Shoppers are invited to join me in reading,
promising a literary event of magnitude,
my book of poetry on Alzheimer's.
"Sets," I say to my partner in reading, "We will read
and give our all to an audience of one or a hundred."

A LITERARY AFTERNOON AT BORDERS

We settle for one.
We sit facing three rows of empty chairs
except for one in the front row, occupied by an employee of Borders,
hoping to be honey to ants. Shoppers walk around the edges,
sneaking looks at Sets and me. "It can't be good if no one's there,"
can almost be read on their faces.

Soon hard rock music fills the room, followed by an aria from an opera
(not even my favorite Puccini), drowning out our voices
as we read our literary creations.
Empty chairs, an aria, poetry without rhyme.
Omar Khayyam, at least had bread and Thou
Beside him. And lots of wine.

Sets, the philosopher, states with conviction,
"I learn something from every experience."
"Yeah, right, Sets," I mumble,
"Empty chairs don't applaud." ✺

THE AUTUMN MOON HANGS

I am poem.
I am ageless.

When I was one and twenty
I spoke of lingering sunsets,
Envied the flight of a solitary bird
That raced the sinking sun
To green nestled leaves.

I am still poem.

The sunset still sinks into the sea,
The solitary bird now sits on a black branch
Plucking red berries above golden leaves.
I am Autumn moon, hanging
Over crayoned fields. Soon, the winter chill.

I am still poem.
I am ageless. ✾

I AM...

I remember when my heart first got broken.
I took my pen and ice-picked that grief
Into a zillion frozen pieces
Until there was nothing left but my poetry.
When that grief got published, I rejoiced and said,
"Grief is good."
I ran myself against arrows, fearless, soared beyond clouds, unafraid.
"This is a poet's life," I said.
Life became a cardiograph, mountain tops and craters.
Distanced from the sound of that staccato beep.
Life was all mine. Grief all my own.
"I am a poet!" I said
Until they stamped Alzheimer's
On my chart. There is no ice pick
Sharp enough to chip my Amyloid plaque.
I'm still a poet, I said.
I am a poet... I said. I said.
I said. ✺

A STRANGER AMONG US

Three young lads walk the mall
Passing my book signing at Barnes & Noble.
One lad breaks away
After turning his head
Toward the book display
On a tripod near me.

"What kind of book is this?
Did you write this?"

"Yes," I say to the lad
Wearing a tiny hoop in one lobe,
A silver stud in his nose.
"This is a book of poems on caregiving."

"I write poems, too. I set them to music.
Do you want to hear one of my poems?"

He rapped his poem in perfect rhythm,
Musical rhymes, poignantly searching
For the meaning of life.

I open my book to offer him
My simple poem, "A Poet's Declaration."

He reads it, looks at me and quietly says,
"You're the first person who understands me."

We talk of how it is
To be a poet...
The aloneness, the pain, the joy.

"No one knows me as you do."
He hands me *Mosaic Moon*,
I sign it, *To Jason*.
"Dammit," I think, after he leaves
To join his two companions
With my book in his hand...
"How did one poem from a stranger
Help him feel there is someone after all,
Who knows and understands him?
How did he recently leave
Thirteen years of school behind him,
A lonely stranger?" ✳

A POET'S DECLARATION

I am a star
In the Milky Way.
I am the crest
On emerald waves.
I am a dewdrop, crystal clear,
Capturing sunbeams in the morning mist.
I am that dust
On butterfly wings.
I am that song
Of a thousand strings.
I am that teardrop
You have kissed.
I am a poet!
I am! I am!
I am that rage
In the thunderstorm.
I am that image
Of a thousand form.
I am magic on each page.
I am a poet!
I am! I am! ❁

DANGEROUS WOMAN

Section II

The Enemy Wears Many Faces

One December morning, my face no longer belonged to me.

Under the rising sun
The enemy came,
Wearing my face.

A new word was also added to my childhood vocabulary that December 7th morning: Jap. Perhaps the shame, fear, humiliation and confusion that followed this word created my passionate awareness that peace, humanity and love must replace fear, hate and ignorance.

Impatience runs throughout these poems. The enemy continues to come, wearing different faces. Hope for peace, justice and equality, and our own humanity continues to remain only rhetoric. Never in my lifetime has this quest become such a loud resounding echo throughout all generations. ✳

POETS FOR PEACE

Each time a poet
Puts pen to paper,
There is a sliver of hope
For Peace. ✾

You promised eons ago,
A world free of battlefields, soldiers,
Children abandoned in fear—in hunger
You offered Hope again and again,

VOICE FROM THE UNBORN

A world, you said, where we stand hand in hand
Beyond color, religion, gender.
You promised a world free of poison,
Clean oceans, earth and air.
"You, the future," you said, "Come to be born.
This world I create for you," you said.

My brothers and sisters believed you.
Now old men and women, they wait.
They wait. Did you hear the unborn?

For eons, you sliced the chrysanthemum
Off its stalk, you left it naked
In the sun.

The ashes of Hiroshima
Were hailed in victory.
Beneath them, my ancestors were buried.

Stop using me, your unborn child.
Promises in meaningless rhetoric
For a not-now future.

I won't wait any longer.
I want to be born,
Today. Promise me. ✤

ABSENCE OF PEACE

Department of Education.
Department of Veterans' Affairs.
Department of Commerce.
Department of Energy.
Department of Homeland Security.
Department of Justice.
Department of Transportation.
Department of Labor.
Department of Interior.
Department of Defense.
(Department of Peace!)
Department of Defense.
(Peace! Peace!)
Department of Defense. ❀

LIVING ON A HYPHEN

"Get off the hyphen"—
A balancing act
Soon after Pearl Harbor.

I slide toward right,
English and shoes, bread and pasta,
Forks, desserts, Frances.

Only for a moment. My face
Slants me to the left,
Sliding, losing grip, hanging.

Hideko, chopsticks, *sushi*,
Rice. Slant eyes. *Miso*.
Pidgin and more rice.

New Year's—to the East
Kadomatsu, mochi.
Sundown—to the West—champagne.

Off balance, the mirror swings—
Japanese-American, a hyphen with two faces
Etched in stone. ✳

When will I know Peace?
"She is at Peace," you said
When my mother died.
Is that the only way I will know Peace?
When I am dead?

WHEN WILL I KNOW PEACE?

You gave me, briefly,
A hummingbird's sip,
On D-Day in 1944.
1953, after the Korean War.
The Vietnam War: 1975

I want to taste it, lick it, swallow it
Like chocolate ice cream in August.
Dripping down my chin, soaking me wet.

I want to hear it, I want to hear it.
What is the sound of Peace?

Wrap it around me,
Wet silk against skin
In three-digit heat.

I want Peace, yes?
No, I want Peace now. Now. ✽

How do you keep your fingers free of dirt?
How do you come in from play without
Mud on your feet, your clothes, your cheeks?
You don't even sweat!

TO CHILDREN OF THE 21ST CENTURY

How do you speak without eye contact
To someone sitting in front of you?
How do you spend time with a friend
Without conversation?

Oh, room filled with the silence
Of families on this holiday.
So mute on this side of the window.
How did you become so mute?

Do you know how rain feels
Soaking your shirt to your skin?
The smell of sea salt in your hair
After a dip in the sea?

Have you watched a little seed
Pushing its head
Out of soil you patted down
A few weeks ago?

Can you see a cardinal, a mynah,
A crow, with your eyes closed, listening
To signature songs sung out to you
In your own back yard?

Do you know the feel of Grandpa's grip
Warm and strong in your hand?
The story behind that long scar that runs
The length of his arm?

Do you carry memories
Of Grandma's smiles
Each time you said,
Hi, Grandma. Can I help you?

Do you ever count clouds, lying
On soft green grass, laughing
Over silly stories, or sharing dreams
With a friend?

Have you wept over a child starving
In Africa or in your neighborhood?
Upset over trees being cut for freeways,
Shopping malls and fancy sports arenas?

Have you ever used the eraser
At the end of a pencil,
Writing a poem, a song, a story.
A thank-you note?

Do you know the feel of crisp
New pages of a book, as they unfold,
Moving plots faster than your impatient
Fingers can follow your eyes?

Oh, Children of the 21st Century,
How did you become so dead? ❀

HOPE

The song is dead.
The swordsman takes
The Victor's stance.

But somewhere still,
A newborn child
Hears the promised song. ✵

THE LAST BOOK

I sit alone under a tree
Turning pages of a book.
Paper sound, delicate
As butterfly wings, the rustle of leaves.
I take the top right corner of each page
Between my thumb and forefinger and savor
Each sound.

"Why are you weeping?" you ask,
With Kindle in hand.
"Because this is the last book on earth."
"A book?" you ask. "What is a book?"
"This is a book," I say, and hand you my book.
"What is this?" you ask.
"That is a bookmark."
I turn to the front of the book.
"Here is an autograph by the author.
She signed this to me in real ink eons ago
At a book signing in a place called a book store." ✺

TO HOMO SAPIENS

I am your forest.
The sound of your ax
Silences my voice.
I am your...
I am...
I...
...

*****

I am Salmon.
I am Black Rhino.
I am Honey Bee.
Soon to be fossilized
Into your earth. Unless

You learn to hear
Hummingbird wings.

HAMBURG, GERMANY

In the Philippines,
WWII followed me into the night.
"Stay indoors after dark, people still remember
Japanese soldiers on Corregidor."

My sixth grader writes in his journal
December 7:
I hate the Japs. I wish they were all dead.
My grandfather told me about them.

In Hamburg, a woman, lined with age,
Holds my hand and weeps to me in German.
I remind her of soldiers from Hawaii.
She has not forgotten their kindness long ago.

Our tears taste the same
In German and in English.
We are the only ones standing
In the aftermath of wars. ✳

Author's Note: The Japanese American soldiers from Hawaii fought in the 100th
Battalion and 442nd Regimental Combat Unit while many of their families
were in internment camps back home.

The signs were there: When students need to talk
they hang around my desk, playing with my stapler or
realigning my pencils and pens until there is privacy
for courage to emerge.

GOLDEN SPIKE

"Sometimes," she quietly started,
still playing with pencils,
"I get up at three in the morning
and hear my dad crying.
I go downstairs and he's sitting
on steps, crying in the dark.
He was in the Vietnam War; he won't talk about it
but I watch him cry a lot. He can't sleep. I know because I always
see him on the steps. I wish I knew how to help him."

Damn! Here's that war again.
No child ought to be wakened at 3 a.m. by a father's tears.
No child ought to be sucked in, to twenty-five-year-old wars.
No child ought to have dreams of brightly crayoned images
Disrupted by black ashes.

I wasn't trained to undo the nature of war.
I didn't know how to banish the phantoms of war.
Maybe...maybe...I gave her a copy of Golden Spike.
"I wrote these poems about the war.
Maybe your dad will find this book helpful."

A few weeks later, in her class journal:
Private to Miss K: My dad is always reading your book.
He carries it around with him and he's not getting up anymore,
He's not crying anymore. Thank you for helping him.
Is it okay if I keep the book a bit longer? He wants to know,
Did you know someone from the Vietnam War?

"Yes," I wrote in her journal,
"Tell your dad I knew someone just like him."

On the last day of school, once again she stood near my desk.
"I'm sorry for not returning your book, but my dad
Is still reading it. I hate to take the book away from him."

"I gave that book to both of you. I'm so glad my poems help him."
She held on to our hug, whispering,
"Thank you, Miss Kakugawa." ✸

Section III

The Fifth Season

I fell in love with a little red wagon when I first learned to read with Dick, Jane, Sally and Tim in their little red wagon. At age six, there was no significance in this attachment, other than my desire to own a similar wagon so I could emulate their lives, which seemed so much richer than mine.

The poems in this section cover the fifth season of my life, represented by that beloved wagon, filled to its brim with poetic evidence of what was and still is. Or, to put it simply, my own aging process. My pen swings into my childhood, then back to the present, sometimes in defiance, sometimes in regret, and often in acceptance and retrospection. And always—that space in that wagon for still another poem.

> *The Red Wagon*
> *Travels over gravel*
> *Bumpity-bump into the night.* ✸

When I am old, my dearest,
Bring me no flannel nightgown,
Long-sleeved with buttons up to my chin.
No house slippers lined with fake fur,

WHEN I AM OLD

Let me feel that cold oak floor under my feet.
I want to feel! I'm not dead yet, you know.

Let me fill the satin of negligee, feel
The red spaghetti strap slipping from my shoulder
While I lay between satin sheets, waiting for you.
(Maybe not satin, I could slip to the floor.)
Whoever told you old is cold
Ought to be hung from that oak.

Come sit with me, even if the cat has my tongue.
Sit and read or do what you do.
Sharing oxygen in silence brings far more joy
Than Q&A on what I had for breakfast.
What does it matter if I remember your name?
Ah, memory. What do we care?

So when I am old,
Just let me be.
Tell a joke, take me to the mall,
Bring me red roses, or better,
A glass of rosé. Laugh with me
For no reason at all. Come,
Let's together—Our Happy Hour. ✳

ON BECOMING 69

How can I be 69 when I feel 49?
How can my mother's daughter turn 69?
For God's sake, children don't age
Not this child, not that way.
How can my mother's daughter turn 69?

Four years ago it began...
With words like *elderly*
Neatly categorized under OLD.
They mailed me funeral plans,
Ads for nursing homes on slick, colored paper
In large black print.
They give me flu shots
Before anyone else, invitations
To free luncheons from
Long-term-care insurance agents.
"You are dying anyway," their messages say.
They probably didn't hear about my 88th birthday
When I plan to make love and listen to leaves
On a windless day. ✽

When I am old and have become
One of the ladies of the Solarium,
Will those quiet nights of padded footsteps
In deserted hallways

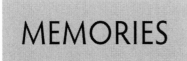

Bring back memories
Of what could have been?
Will fragments of those memories
Resound louder than the hushed voices
Of nurses' aides returning
To haunt me in my aloneness?

Memories...
Of that stranger in Wyoming
Looking under the hood of my car,
Looked at me just as carefully and said,
"I could fix this by tonight
But won't you stay?"
Oh, how I wanted to stay.
But I said no, and what I denied
Accompanied me home.

I can't forget that night.
He refused to charge me for his work
And quietly said, instead,
"Get in your car and go. Just go."
"Why," I asked, and then I knew
When his boss, belly over his belt
Came yelling, "Charge her!"
I had said no to him
Just a few hours before.

Memories...
Of the man who bought me chocolate ice cream
Outside Costco.
How we talked and laughed,

Licking our ice cream cones,
Two strangers, without names
So connected, so familiar.
I ached to finish this scene
Produced so many times
In novels and films.

But I said no.

Memories...
Of a stranger in Florence
Who screeched his truck,
As I walked nonchalantly down the street
In my new white hat,
"You speak English?
You and me,
We go dancing, tonight?"
He danced around me
Holding an imaginary me in his arms,
I said, "No, no speak English."

Then there was that young Italian in Venice
Who held my hand and said I was beautiful.
"Come with me to the Lido."
I withdrew my hand from his,
That summer evening in the piazza.
My chain-linked imagination, me floating—
Another tourist face down in the canal.

Memories... ✸

Ah, sweet babe, born tonight,
Stop your crying and listen well.
There's no crown on your head,
And your mother's breast is dry.

FROGS AND KISSES DON'T MAKE A PRINCE

But listen, babe, born tonight,
Listen to my song.

Wise men say you're born a prince
And wise men seldom lie.
If a crown makes you a prince,
You can be stolen by a thief.
Crowns don't make princes, babe,
But the soul that's free to be.
Princes smile and princes laugh,
Princes feel and princes weep.
Princes fear and princes love,
Princes grow and princes flow
With or without a golden crown.

Wise men say there are witches.
Beware of witches, little babe.
Their voices sing like mother's milk,
They come to you when you are dry.
They sing to you for your soul
And for the prince you are tonight.

Ah, sweet babe, born tonight,
Beware of witches and their song.
If their song becomes your song
And you give your soul away,
By the pond you'll croak all night
Catching flies for your joy.

Ah, sweet frog, by the pond.
Stop your tears and listen well.
You were born a prince one night,
Until you sang the witches' song.

Wise men say you're still a prince,
And wise men seldom lie.
You gave your soul away that day
When you sang the witches' song.
Stop, don't waste your life away,
Searching for a maiden's kiss.
Those kisses are a myth, sweet frog.

Ah, sweet babe, born tonight,
Love and feel and always be.
Be the prince you're born tonight,
Kisses don't make princes, babe.
Princes make their princes. ✿

how regrettable to be almost all-knowing, matured and wise.
after decades of life, how very disheartening
to be so cemented to one's own existence, that sense and reason
become the forum for all who come, those unexpected guests
from the back alleys of my youth.

WINDS OF THE YOUNG

but to be there once again,
to be whipped by the winds,
back and forth and any which way.
to be that youth facing the world
believing life is for saying yes, yes, yes,
the doors unlocked for entries and exits.

how lamentable to have come to this stage in life,
locked and rooted to the most of it.
how mortifying to be so wizened with age,
to begin each day aware of consequences
instead of edges.

oh, but to step off the irrepressible, to be unafraid,
tossing caution to the winds,
to live as erasable pencil #2
instead of permanent liquid blue,
to be almost unknown.

ah yes, I was there:
it was there my heart got broken,
when my poetry got written,
I flew with wings, without
feet or sense of the ground.

then I grew up.
or did I grow old? ❀

THE GENERATION GAP

The weathered old man
Applauds the stripling
Whose young limbs sway and whip
In the harsh winds.

It was not long ago
When the weathered old oak
Had fought the same furious storm,
Dying and rebirthing, dying and rebirthing
Until birth itself
Became stronger than death. ✦

He stands on the rock
Of Gibraltar's fame
To stretch his reach
To carve his name.

GOING HOME

He whittles and whittles
Each curve, each line,
His tongue follows suit
Across his lips.
His art complete, he steps aside
To marvel at his feat.
The forest shouts his name, his name,
High above the towering sky.

He returns to his name
Forty years hence,
Stands in silence
Before his altar.
He drops to his knees
To feel his name
Now invisible to the naked eye.
The wind, the birds, whisper pass
Singing songs without his name.
He looks for the rock
That once held him high—
Now a stone beneath the moss
Between his black Gucci shoes. ❋

She sat on the porch,
A two-year-old, shyly
Looking at the world,
And fills it with confusion.

THE PORCH

The red train station, trains
Transporting sugar cane and passengers,
The constant flow of strangers,
Strangers waiting for trains,
Train engineers and conductors
Dropping in for a glass of water.
The constant motion of people
Like ants on a picnic spread.
She sat and watched until
Confusion chased her back
Into the safety of her home.

Years later, now a teen.
The porch, a place of solitude
Surrounds her with romance novels
And girlhood dreams.
The estranged station, replaced
By a post office, continues
Its buzz of people like bees
Darting in and out of hives.
The porch, an entryway to her mother's
Dressmaker's shop.

On weekends, a Visitors' Information Center:
Tourists stopping by for directions
To the famed Warm Springs.
When disrupted too often,
She puts her romantic dreams aside
And escapes into the house.

Throughout the years,
It was still her favorite place.
The porch, two steps from the ground,
Now rose seven more steps
After Madame Pele handed out
A fiery eviction notice, and
Forced the evacuation of family
And house to a new locale.
Greeted now by two large banyans,
Guarded by Ohi'a trees,
Carpeted below by red ginger flowers.
A gardenia bush she planted years ago,
White ginger blossoms from plants rooted up
From roadsides, transplanted for her view from the porch.
Finches, sparrows, cardinals and noisy mynahs
Steal silences. It was still her porch.

She sits on a wooden rocking chair,
A mug of coffee in hand,
Her first Winston cigarette,
Her poems of first and lost love—
Lady Chatterley's Lover, Fanny—
X-rated books in concealed covers
In her place of privacy.

Four years ago, her mother's stroke—
A wrap-around ramp transforming the porch
Along with her mother and her place
On the porch.

Today she returns to the empty house.
She sits on the porch on a plastic chaise lounge chair,
A mug of coffee from a neighbor's house.
The ramp obstructs her views
To tree tops, clouds and skies.
The porch, just a porch,
The house, just a house.
Without her mother in residence,
It is no longer home.
There is no return—no porch.
There is no porch. ✳

GRANDMA'S HOUSE

It was a house for grandkids,
A place, screen doors never closed,
Offering you a world in waiting
Unobstructed, without walls,
Rules or strings.

It was a place you could be
The person hidden.
Without pretense, truth and freedom
Ruled your visit.
A place where you could nap
On the old faded couch,
Talk story around the kitchen table,
Sit on the back steps with cousins and kin
Or simply take a quiet walk
Around the neighborhood.

It was a house that welcomed you over the years,
In all stages of your life
From childhood to boyfriends,
Husbands and offspring.
It was always a place without rules
Except for one:
"Eat, be happy and come again." ✳

A final look
In the rear-view mirror
At the house where I was born.
The rooms now silent,

THE HOUSE

Emptied of voices, footsteps,
laughter, life.
Walls bare of collected history,
Some buried in the backyard.

The faucets no longer run,
The kitchen no longer sends
Aromas through screen windows.
The clotheslines hang loosely,
All slid to the right of the mirror
Along the edge of the driveway.

Old wooden clothespins
Like dentures from an old man's smile
Hold on to nothing, nothing at all.
No flapping of sheets, no nightgowns
In the sun-swept breezes.
Silence. My unsmiling face
Falls off the edge of the mirror.

The sparrows cling to a branch,
Like clothespins on the line.
The house hangs on to life,
And slowly vanishes
In a last backward glance. ✤

I sit at my favorite table in my coffee-shop cave,
A cup of coffee in one hand, a pen in the other.
My scenic view, the parking lot.
Each tree-sheltered space, occupied,
In this three-digit heat.

MAKE ME CRY, WORLD

Soon there is movement. A woman with walker,
osteoporosis humped on her back, snails her way
toward a sedan. Her drop foot scuffing the pavement,
leaving a trail of spilled orangeade. Her granddaughter
opens the doors, and waits for her. And waits.

The woman knows the dance. She turns her walker around,
two steps from the door, inches her way, backside toward the seat,
pauses and offers her arms to her granddaughter. Both dance
    the light fandango.
Granddaughter gently and gingerly tugs at her sleeve,
removes the jacket off her back.

Beads of sweat shine on her face, granddaughter wipes her brows.
They share a smile before the walker is stored in the back,
Grandmother in a light, flowered cotton blouse is led to the
    front seat.

I snap the seatbelt, the engine turns.
Images of my past light up the walls of my cave.
My mother and I danced that dance.
Tears down my face, like the ink in my pen,
continue the story of kindness and smiles. ✽

i am an overnight guest
in their brand-new home,
    both girls, instead of pulling straws,
    sleep with me
        on their king-sized bed
            with me sandwiched in the middle

OVERNIGHT GUEST

giggles, giggles, betwixt the sheets,
    "go to sleep!" "stop poking me!"
        bring more giggles
            but even giggles soon get sleepy.

brandi is sound asleep on my right,
    nicole on my left slides to the edge,
        proclaiming, "i love to sleep near the edge."

i curve one arm around her,
    holding her in from the edge
        before she falls like icarus
            into total darkness.

i lie awake, thinking of life,
    how some of us live near the edge
        taking risks, pursuing dreams, living
            outside of little white boxes,
                often teetering on one foot.

only in childhood do we know,
     someone's arm is always there,
          holding us from the edge.

and this is how it ought be
     when we are young and trusting
          in our mother's home. ✳

WANTED: WORDS

"Call me when you land."
The words yet to be invented
To reach across that moment.

Arms laden with bags, she turns,
Her wriggling fingers, unspoken sentences.
"Good-bye."

On the day she took her first breath,
Eighteen years ago, silence,
To hold in those words not yet invented.

Someday she will seek
The same un-invented words
At airports or train stations.

"Call me when you land."
"Have you got everything?"
"Good-bye." ❀

"We will need a biopsy,"
He tells me matter-of-factly
Looking straight into my eye.
"It may be cancer."

CANCER?

Cancer? How dare you
Say cancer.

Why not something
Vague and unclear,
"Abnormal cell growth" or
Why not, "Probably nothing's wrong
But we'll take tests anyway."
Damn you! How dare you
Say cancer
And look me
Straight in the eye.

Lie to me, you bastard!

He is waiting
For me to speak.

I say nothing.
I look at him straight
In the eye.
Cancer? ✳

Like lightning bolts,
He sizzles d-e-a-t-h
Upon my back.

PROGNOSIS: CANCER

Why didn't you lie
When I said
I wanted the truth?
The Artist
In his Gallery
Pinpoints
My imperfection
On the screen.
Are you sure
You know my name?
A statistician
Drops a number
Into my womb.
If I smile
Will he wake me
From his lies?
The Arctic Wind
Chills and freezes.
Fire to Ice. Fire to Ice
I promise to be good.
I don't want to die.

Ice. ✻

SURGERY

As white knights
Gather around me
I think sadness:

> If I should die
> No one in this immaculate room
> Will shed a tear
> For me,
> My heart and lungs,
> And my uterus
> Anonymous
> As a faceless stranger
> In a crowd.
>
> These white knights
> Circling, lying.
> They cannot hear
> My rage against
> This anonymity.
>
> I did rage
> Against this black
> Night. ✸

"This will sting a little,"
The anesthetist soothingly says.
"This will make you drowsy."
Slowly, I begin to lose control,

WHERE ARE THE PRETTY THOUGHTS?

My feelings and thoughts begin to drift.
How many times has he said that to patients
Who hear it for the first time?
Who ball up in a knot?
I open my eyes, heavy with sleep
The ceiling waving above me.
The thought of dying
Enters my mind.
"I may never come out of this,"
Panics my breathing,
My insides trembling,
Slowly crawls out of my skin
Up my arms and inner thighs.
God, I'm so terribly alone and frightened.
Who can help me?
No one, not a mother, not a lover, not my best friend.

Think pretty thoughts.
Pretty thoughts. What are pretty thoughts?
Meadows with brooks? Birds? Flowers?
Christmas trees. Yes, Christmas lights.
The trees go on sale tomorrow.

Or my students, perhaps. Please, let me see their faces.
The tightening getting tighter.
Tomorrow. Tomorrow.
I'll be in my own bed, laughing this.
I'll be sharing this idiotic fear with anyone.
Tomorrow, I'll do that.
But tomorrow is not here.
Pretty thoughts. Pretty thoughts.

The chills and trembling continue.
Can I ask him to stop? Right, just stop.
Another shot. I'm drowsy.
Losing consciousness,
Hearing the muffled voices of
White Knights circling the
Cold table.
Pretty thoughts.

I don't want to die. ✸

THE VERDICT

"There is no malignancy."
He looks me straight
In the eye.
I say nothing.
I look at him
Straight in his eye
And I smile and smile
And I smile.

"At least none
that we could see."
You bastards. ✻

Our kitchen was always open
To neighbors, friends, the lonely and all the homeless
But there was no Pepsi.

THE KITCHEN

Grubby little me wanting a Pepsi
Knew where to go.
Fanny's kitchen.

I'd sit on her porch
For her to notice me.
Waiting for her voice:

"Oh, Hideko,
I neva see you. So hot today,
You want some Pepsi?"

I'd nod and follow her to the kitchen
where she poured it warm
In an aluminum mug.

I sipped and felt warm Pepsi
Flow down my parched throat.
Both hands on the mug.

There was no ice in our village,
No electricity, no supermarkets,
Deprivation was bliss.

I hear the dialogue
between Fanny and her children:
"Ma, what happened to the Pepsi?"

"Oh, the Kakugawa girl was here again
So I wen give it to her."
"Oh man, she always here, drinking our Pepsi."

When I became a caregiver
I sought refuge in Fanny's kitchen again...
She was gone then.

Oh, how I needed that Pepsi,
Living half in fear in the eerie world
Called my mother's Alzheimer's.

Using Kapoho-girl savvy
I found solace in a new kitchen, Jane's.
She was Fanny in every respect.

Her door always unlocked,
I'd go straight to her kitchen.
"I need a mother," I'd say.

"I dropped my mother at adult care
And I'm tired and hungry."
That brought Jane to her feet.

Brewed decaf coffee,
Lunch or breakfast, dessert,
More decaf while I kept an eye on the clock.

I can almost hear my mother saying,
"Hideko, eat, eat. You look too skinny."
There is something so motherly about those words.

Again, I hear the same conversation at the end of Jane's day,
With family gathered around the dinner table.
"Ma, what happened to last night's leftover dinner?"

"Oh, Fran was here today."

Jane died last week. I grieve
For the kitchen, no matter what time of day,
And for her mothering when I needed it most.

There's a kitchen in Sacramento.
A kitchen with another name,
But all the same kitchen.

Mary's kitchen is where I sit
When the need for a mother and a friend is greatest.
When a kitchen is needed.

I sit and wait for freshly brewed decaf coffee,
Or hot green tea with homemade snacks,
Among oak trees and humming birds.

I honor all three women tonight,
A kitchen without lock and warm Pepsi
That soothes our parched throat. ✺

A house unpainted:
A corrugated roof, four walls.
A floor, six by two-and-a-half.
A redwood seat with two round holes

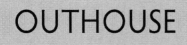
OUTHOUSE

Sized to fit two adult bottoms
Balanced on used railroad ties
Squared over a bottomless pit.
Here she sits and answers
Nature's call.

The fear of falling
Turns her knuckles white
As she holds on to the edge
Of the wooden seat.

It's a generic outhouse,
Unlike the neighbor's
Where their additional hole,
Though smaller,
Makes it a throne for three.

A wooden box against a wall,
Filled with red, square wrappers
Greets her with faint apple scent.
At arm's reach, torn sheets of
The Hilo Tribune Herald
Hang on a nail.
On the floor, a back-up supply,
Sears and Montgomery Ward,
Her Charmin.

Outside the door, a peach tree
Reaches toward the sky.
During the season

When in bloom,
The scent of peach petals
Loses to the stench.
No flies, no gnats, except for cockroaches
Dwell below, sometimes over her butt.

Dampness and heat create unspeakable odor
In a stranger's outhouse.
She gags and holds her breath
In other outhouses,
Races home when the need arises.
Home, Sweet Home.

Above all, it is her place of refuge,
A place where her need
For undisturbed solitude
Is unquestioned.

It is a place where she sits and reads
Books, comics, *True Confessions*
Cover to cover, along with gulps
Of *Life in These United States.*

When called to do the dishes
Or to start the rice,
She shouts from this redoubt, "I stay in da toilet!"
It is a refusal she has perfected
After years of practice, respected
By neighbors and passers-by.
What parent would dare call the Empress' daughter
When Nature's Call came first?
It was the House of Royalty. ❀

My first Michigan summer,
Kay and I, two mad women,
turned the kitchen into a canning factory:

TWO MAD CANNERS

Pickled cucumbers, bread & butter, dill.
Christmas-colored watermelon rind pickles,
peaches, pears, corn relish, rhubarb, tomatoes.

Like two librarians, we filled the basement shelves
until there was no space for a salt shaker or
Hemingway's *Old Man and the Sea.*

In the freezer, airtight: strawberries, blueberries,
corn, squash, beans, zucchini, tomatoes
zucchini, carrots, zucchini.

We captured Abundance
to the sound of "Pop!" the High Five
for the two mad canners.

Come Winter's end,
I step down, to the basement,
with Empty Shelf Syndrome.

Our summer's work thinning
with each trip down the stairs—
A jar of watermelon pickles. ✲

SOUNDS OF OLD PLANTATION DAYS

I miss the sound of the trucks tonight
Hauling cane through old sugar towns.
Not the bounce and rattles of the empties,
As they head back to the fields
Over the twists of narrowing country roads.
It's the dull muffled thump of trucks
Laden with tons of fresh sticky cane
That pass through my silent, sleepless thoughts.
I'm not alone on these nights,
In the company of faces sitting high
In darkened cabs, the glow of half-burnt cigarettes
Hanging from their lips like summer lanterns. ✤

Yes, my love,
I know.

SHIKATA-GA-NAI*
AND I MUST GO

The garden needs
    watering.
The rose bush needs
    pruning.
The lawn needs
    mowing,
Cutworms are
    feasting.

But someone is calling
And I must go now.

The washer's on rinse,
The dishes need drying.
The weeds are jousting
In-between the radishes.
But I'm distracted,
Someone is calling.

My novel's half written,
        Chapters without climax.
        Poems without words
        Lingering in my head.
        All brushed aside by demands
        I cannot ignore.

So listen, love, before I go,
Weep if you must but not for long.
See what I've done and let me go.
He calls my name—
Shikata-ga-nai. ❁

*It cannot be helped; it's in fate's hand.

SEASONS

It was a time of innocence...
Sitting on our beds in college dorms,
Not questioning the nature of the universe
Or of mankind. Our questions
Nowhere to be found in college texts.
"What kind of car do you want
Your next boyfriend to have?"
"A sports car," I said, "preferably red."
"A truck," said someone, born in Michigan.
"And how about children?"
We sat naming our children
Without chromosomes and only half their DNA.

The seasons have come and gone
And once again there are questions.
Not of the nature of things
But of our own mortality.
"Which of us will go first?" ❀

Section IV

Collected Poems
from Four Published Books

My best-laid plans to become a writer were simply plotted: Support myself as a teacher. Retire at age fifty-five. Write that great American novel. Now all I had to do was let Providence do her work.

My first book of poetry was published when I was in my 30s. The gods were fast-forwarding my plans. Clearly, this was a sign that I was to have a very short life. I had to live fast and fearlessly. Within six years, four poetry books bore my name. I was ready to die. Fifty years later, I am still here.

Those earlier poems speak of that period that gave us the Vietnam War, the Age of the Free Spirit, struggles against racism and my own personal quest to seek love and my own womanhood. There are still wars, broken soldiers, human inequality and injustice today. My search for self, love, joy and meaning in life continues. Who would have thought poems written in my youth would still speak to us today?

Poems in this section come from *Sand Grains* (1970), *White Ginger Blossom* (1971), *Golden Spike* (1973) and *Path of Butterflies* (1976).

Enjoy. ✻

Selected Poems from

SAND GRAINS

Silently I watch
Him walk from me;
My life, my love
In his hands.

UNTITLED

Then I see him
Carelessly fling
His open palms
Toward the sea.

Quietly I kneel
To pick up shells,
Dried and broken
Against my flesh.
Shells that once,
Quivering with life,
Were warm and soft
To every touch.

Silently I see
Him walk away
To another tomorrow—
Another shore.
Free from promises; like the wind
Tossing sand grains
In my eyes.

Good-bye. ❀

FALLING

Little girl...alone
With little girls' dreams,
Passing puddles, pebbles and shores.

Safe from falls and little bruised knees,
Little girls' dreams
Keep her free.

Little girl...gone
Swept into sea,
Tears on her cheeks, pain in her heart.
A hundred fears, yet not afraid.
A woman, a woman
No longer free. ✹

BOY INTO MAN

I hold his hand
And softly cry

Not yet, not yet.

But even little boys
Need to be free.

I feel him slip
Away from me—

Tiny, scrubby, enormously brave.

And without a glance
To where I stand,

He enters the room
Alone. ❀

YOURS TRULY

Deep inside of me
Lies a woman
Waiting to be seen
By passersby.
So many travelers
Yet each passes on
Unseeing, unknowing
The woman hidden
Deep inside of me.
You who stop and
See me here
Deep within these
Seemingly simple woods,
Travel on to wavering lights
Leaving behind
The woman I am;
Waiting to be found
Once again
In this world of
Superficial
Blindness ✷

UNDRESSING IN THE NIGHT

I'm lonely. I cried
And walked the nights
But could not find
A friend to touch.

Until one night
On the mirrored wall
I saw myself.
From within each glow
And in my presence
I became
My true naked self. ✸

UNTITLED

I saw six buds,
Counted roses
Instead.

But the
Bugs got
To them
First ❀

NO GREEN STAMPS FOR REDEMPTION

I shopped
And sought
Endlessly
For one
Special item
Marked
"For Sale."

I could not
Find what I
Sought,
But the spree
Was fun in spite of
The signs—
"Not for Sale." ✺

ALIENATION

I sit and watch
Each passerby
And see not people,
But painted faces
Framed and fenced
Like canvassed Picassos.
Each to another,
A colored brush
On surfaced lines,
Unseeing, unfeeling
The hidden soul
Behind each smile.
A gallery of faces,
Cold, hard, yet
Highly prized
For each painted stroke. ❀

I feel thee enter
And time stands still
As thou comes in thine suit
Of steel and shield,

FROM AN INTRUDER

Cold and hard
Betwixt us both.
Thou taketh a drink
From my flowing cup.
Thou taketh it fast,
Hot, steaming,
Bitter and black,
Refusing my spoon
Of sugar and cream.

I wonder now
As I hear thee leave
How it would be
To have thee here,
Stripped of thy suit
Of protective shine,
Vulnerable to intruders
Such as I,
Penetrating beyond
Thine naked self.
I wonder then
How thou would take
This cup I offer
Thee today. ❋

A HAPPENING

A touch
A look
A smile

And that has made
All the difference
In the world,
As my heart
So gently touched
Is lifted to
The cloudless sky. ✾

LESS THAN FOREVER

After it was over
He unsmilingly left me
Transitory
Dreams
And
Illusive
Images
For me to keep
In memory's box.

That
Was
All. ✽

CONSUMMATION

I didn't mind dying
The night I was touched.
You held me so close
And whispered love.
I didn't mind dying
As my heart over-filled
Beyond any verse
Could ever reveal
The merging of two
In silent love.

Now as I walk
The empty shores,
Hearing the cry
Of each lonely wave,
I don't mind dying
Once again. For though I die
So many times,
I live each hour
After dark with
Each setting sun. ✳

ON A SEPTEMBER MORNING

Speak not of
Broken promises,
Of drifting sand
And waves,

For time was all
That was granted to us
That endless
Summer day ✻

MEMORY

Till rippling breezes
Can be seized,
And children's laughter stopped,
I know my soul
Will never free
The memory of you. ✻

MORNING GLORIES

Rainbows, Camelots
Like mornings glories at noon
Short-lived! Folded! Gone!

The world overflows
With morning glories at morn,
Empty cups at dusk ✤

KITE

After the heavy winds
Hurtling down to the cold ground
The soaring kite falls ✤

DEWDROPS

All too soon are gone
Dewdrops on the morning lawn
Swallowed by One above. ✿

FALL

Golden brown flurries
Whimsically, tenderly fall,
Carpet of delight. ✿

TEACH ME TO LEAVE EMPTY SHELLS ON LONELY BEACHES

Like water lilies unfolding
Toward each morning's warmth,
I am found once again
In the silence of the night,
Rising above the tears of yesterday's dreams.

Who would have thought
Empty shells on lonely beaches
Could be filled once again
With each rising tide. ✣

The mother wave rose up, gently nudged,
And seeing hesitancy, lovingly spanked
The piece of driftwood that longed to
Remain between each swell out in the
Midst of everything-ness—and by so
Doing, sent it back to a familiar shore—
A shore each grain of sand, each rock,
Each tree needs. That driftwood, like
The mother wave, knows it will be washed
Ashore and beached.

RISING TIDES

But wait!
High tides and ocean storms
Can reach all shores.
That mother wave can beckon
And the driftwood is once again
Out to sea....

But the driftwood, spanked back to shore,
No longer afloat in the moving sea, lodges
Itself in the familiar sand—giving each
Living creature, each growing plant, life
And shelter. It does not hear her beckoning
Call to return once again into the tranquility
Of her swells. The mother wave longs to be-
Come part of another shore—part of each
Little grain of sand that surrounds and
Warms that little driftwood. She cries
To touch ashore but the sea around her
Slaps her....No!

And the mother wave knows...she is a part
Of a wave greater than one, a current
Stronger than both...she does not
Move in the great big sea alone. She
Can only wait for that rising tide.
Feelingly, longingly, she sends little
Currents back to shore. "Let each little
Ripple, each little tear loosen each grain
Of sand." But little ripples, silent tears
Do not free a sanded wood.

Other driftwoods, other shores quietly
Dwell in depths unknown. Touched by one
Special driftwood to her naked core, the
Mother wave knows other driftwoods, other
Shores will be felt but never touched.

The mother wave grows and swells with each
Little cloudburst, each little teardrop,
As she awaits the return of her beloved
Driftwood.

Wait...wait...
For one thunderous cloudburst,
One rising tide.
Rise, Oh Storms!
Rise, All Tides!

Wait...wait... ❋

REFLECTION

Do little fallen sparrows
Damningly, painfully cry
Of short-lived flights
Over silver foiled lakes
And crayoned fields;

Or do little fallen sparrows
Happily, gratefully whisper
– I flew –

As dusk slowly turns its head
And dry dead leaves
Lightly touch their statued backs? ✤

To the mountain or the sea
I heard him call,
Then saw them swarm toward the rise.
A mountain is forever

MORE THAN A MOUNTAIN

I heard one say:
Stable, still and safe.
Come, let us seek
The inherited peak.
I stood away from the
    conventional pack
And silently walked toward the sea.

I felt instead each gentle wave
Slowly moving in on me
Bringing shells and driftwood to my flesh
For me to touch and feel and know.
Then out to sea, all gone again
Till the next rising tide.

Were I to live a hundred years
I'd leave the mountain for the sea
And live each hour like each wave,
Free and moving, shore to sea.
And when the hundredth year arrives
I'd leave the gift given me
And quietly leave the many shores,
The many seas I had come to know.
For when that hundredth year arrives,
The mountain too, I must leave.
Had I sought the stable crown,
I would have known one mountain, one peak—
And living, living, is less than forever,
Is for today. ❀

UNTITLED

Each step a footprint, yet
Had I feared backward glances,
I would have been nowhere
Nowhere at all.... ✿

ABORTED

On Pegasus Wings
I take flight,
Wrapped in sheets
Of *Sand Grains*,*
Enraptured, captured
By created bliss.
I soar on high
In timeless flight.

Abruptly I fall
Off Pegasus Wings.

I feel the wind
Awaken my flesh,
All tethered reins
Wrenched from my hold.
Aborted now of
Ephemeral joy,
I cry out, "No!
Not yet!"
As each sheet possessed,
Falls into earthly hands.

* The title of my first published book of poetry.

Selected Poems from

WHITE GINGER BLOSSOM

WHITE GINGER

Unfolding into fragrance
For one breathless moment
White Ginger blossom. ✾

LIFE

Hit me!
Kill me!
Love me!

He does not hear.
He brushes my cheek
Lightly, soberly whispers

Live—
Give—
Be—

Then steps aside. ✳

DAMNATION

I wait for you to take this gift
I've so preciously kept for you.
But you let each hour pass
Silently, silently—still.
You wait till I am stripped
Of my soul, my smile, my self.
Then you leave me standing here
Cold, completely nude
A naked fool.

Forgive the truth
I offered you
When I said
I love you.
I
Love
You. ✳

ARMORED KNIGHT

Without a glance
To see what he's touched,
He moves through the woods
Like the wind
Leaving behind one tender leaf
Torn and shaken by his
Passing slice. ✻

You bring me
Plastic flowers to reap
And say this is all
That will keep.
You look at me

With painted eyes
And swear you see me
True and deep.
You hold me in
Your sculptured arms
Touch me with
Your silent lips
All by fluorescent
Moonlight.

TO A SCULPTURED LOVER

A sculptured world's
An easy world
Chiseled out of
Changing times.
Free from tears
And pain and love
Artfully made for
Hammered souls.
But I was born
Of sweat and tears
And love and pain
And thus will seek
A heart that cries
Close to mine
Into mine.

Were you not
Born long ago
Of the womb
Such as mine?
Or have you not
Been born at all? ✳

TWENTY STRINGS

I watch him move and entertain
Laughter, joy and skill.
Cleverly moves from ring to ring
Thunderous applause continuously rains
Deafening the bill of each artful kill
With each performance he knowingly brings.

After each act, he lies silent on stage.
Safe, contented, he grins and observes
As each leaves—with whispered encores.
"I move not by will nor love nor rage
But by twenty strings held by One who serves."
And thus lives he—by such lore.

Thus say all performers alike
Puppets all by One above.
Know they not the pain and tears
Of one who lives naught by strings
But heart and soul and—truth? ✿

DANGER: BOY AT PLAY

He skipped about
The little girl
Knocking down
Castles in the sand.
With each kick
A thousand dreams
Dispersing into
Nothingness.
And when she tried
To enter his
He stood and would not
Let her in.
For this was his
His very own
Closed to intruders
Such as she.

Be aware
Oh, little girl,
Of little games
Boys play. ✽

I walk through
The slush of melting snow
And feel each icy wave
Seep through every

A WATERY GRAVE

Inch of me.
I try to remember
The world yesterday
When it quietly came
The sphere of poetry and song—
As each little snowflake
Covered each barren soil
Blanketing the world
In stillness and peace.

I cry to remember
When hearts met together
And souls walked hand in hand
Through the silent world of two.
I try to remember
But feel instead
The muddy wet
Of winter's end.

I close my eyes
To the watery grave
And dream of tomorrow
When each oozing flow
Breaks into spears of
Crocuses and song.
But the frigid river
Is all I feel
As I lose the world
That was once a poem
And what could be
Another song. ✾

MY SON

He allowed him
To be born
Of my womb.
He allowed me
To hold him
Close.
To love him,
To know him.

He did not allow me
To see him die. ✼

HOPE

He emptied my page
Of dried kept petals
And left me instead
A new budding green
Of promised roses. ✼

DEATH, BE GENTLE

Let me reach out gently
And blow each glowing candlelight.
For when night falls with my breath
Morning seems so very close,
Warm and peaceful
As one's eyes to the soul.

Let me call night in
For morning seems so far away
When darkness suddenly falls on you
Without a warning, without a glance.

Let me know when night comes.
Bring me each candlelight. ✾

DO NOT ENTER

So many signs along my way
Of Detours and Stops and One-Way Only.
Had I heeded each stenciled stop
I would have been everywhere
Yet nowhere at all.

I have traveled roads forbidden by man,
Played in fields of dandelion weeds.
Have felt Christmas in warm July,
Left footprints in sand untouched in June.
And driven on gravel warned Danger! Stop!

The bruises, falls, the bloody cuts,
The loneliness of a traveler alone.
These I treasure, these I feel
Now that I've returned
To where I began
So many years ago. ✸

KANSAS CITY, USA

Immaculate white boxes
Along shimmering green elms
Line the streets of this Midwestern town.
Where Sunday worshippers
Swear and live
On brotherhood and love
One solemn hour, one hour a week.
And till that next churchly hour
Fly the flag to
Proudly display
Kansas City, USA. ✽

A GIFT FROM MAN

A breathless film of man's ingenuities
Quietly hovers over his city.

Where he came from
I do not know
For I was asleep
When he arrived.
Uninvited, unwanted
Unexpectedly he came.
So unaware of him was I
Until I felt his breath on mine.
And though I beg him
To leave my side,
He sits and waits
And knowingly smiles,
"You made me come;
I'm here to stay."
And slowly closes
In on me. ✽

HIS BROTHER'S KEEPER

In the peaceful
Hour of the sandman
The piercing sound
Of the siren
Rushing—speeding—
To one helpless soul
Somewhere in the streets
Of this American town.

It's part of their job
You see,
And they get paid. ✾

a grain of sand, a lighted coal
lonely nights, a cup of coffee
stokely carmichael.

THE HUMAN RACE

sizzling sunset
a lava flow
an autumn day
thanksgiving.

ginger blossom
a banana split
lighted candle, a spicy scent
the orient, spring.

cotton candy
crested waves
drifting snow in early morn
columbus.

chocolate fudge
a firewood
hawaiian eyes
a glass of beer.

Each a color in its right
Yet not a rainbow in sight.
Till each stands hand in hand
Across the cerulean sky. ✹

A RESTAURANT SCENE

A pizza and a beer
And a smile in between
Such a simple order
For a relationship. ✾

RAINDROP

A single raindrop
Joined by seven, one and two,
A watery stream. ✾

ME

I can hardly be seen
Among the mountains and the clouds.
Just a tiny speck, obscure and small.

Yet I exist.
I exist. ✻

IDENTITY

Lost and found in
Forests.

Snowdrifts
Puddles
And beaches

One can be beautiful.

A leaf
A snowflake
A raindrop
A pebble. ✻

A RUDE AWAKENING

Smoothed and shaped
By wind and wave
They lie like children
Peacefully asleep.
Undisturbed pebbles
On the shore.
I step on top them
All alike
Until I stop
And turn each face.
I see instead
Each jagged wound
Beneath each
Faceless, nameless stone.
Shaped and shaved
By wind and wave.
I step between them
Now treasured souls
Deeply asleep
For
My
Awakening. ✼

A SPECIAL TOUCH

Had she not come
That quiet morn
To gently lift me
From my grave,
I would have lived
Unnoticed, unknown,
Insignificantly imbedded
In the sand,
An ordinary log.
But she came
To where I lay
And touched me softly
With both hands.
Tenderly brushed
Each grain of sand
Off my crusted dying soul.
And as she turned me
Lovingly over
She made me
A driftwood.
A special driftwood. ❀

WITH THINE EYES

A look
If it's right
Can hold and bind,
Warm and love,
Caress and feel,
And touch and say
What poets have said
Since "Grecian Urn."
This look
If it's right
Can sing the songs
Since Virgil's time
And fill your heart and soul
And mine. ✸

I stand alone
And watch the waves
And know not what
Each brings to me.

REVELATION

I pick a rose
In morning's light
And wonder why
The fragrant dew.

I hear the sound
Of a laughing child
But the song he sings
Comes silent to me.

But when your flesh
Touches mine
I know what life's
Mystery holds.

I know what each wave
Brings to me
And why the fragrant life.
I hear the world
Fill with song
Of each coming child.
When your flesh
Touches mine. ✾

SHHHHHHH

Love comes in many voices
Sometimes loud and distinct
Like a lizard's mate call
Late at night.
Sometimes soft and slow
Soothingly still like moondrops
Tossed on shimmering seas.
Sometimes love whispers past
Our vibrating world
Lost like a pulse midst the sounds
Of a thousand strings.

Listen. ✿

3 A.M.

As the world
Empties into sleep
I wonder why
For some of us
It's mountain tops
And valley greens,
Sky-bound jets
And subway trains.

Never in between. ✹

A POET'S SONG

If the pen
The tongue
And the heart
Filled the air
With one song
What a symphony of truth! ✺

Selected Poems from

GOLDEN SPIKE

Each
Word
He
Sends

UNABRIDGED
LOVE

I
See
Them
All,
In
Oxford,
Webster's,
Unabridged
Et al.

Yet
I
Think
Each
Word
I
Read
Was
Written
By
His
Hand
For
Me.

Love
You
I
Joy
You
Bring. ❀

When he was six
Away from home,
He pledged allegiance
To the flag

POW

For equality, justice
And freedom for all.

Then at twenty
He took his gun,
Dragged his friends
From instant fire.

He shot to kill
So we could fly
The Red, the White,
The beautiful Blue.

Aged twenty-six
He returns in blue,
To the cheers of voices
Welcome Home, POW.
A limp in his walk,
Grey in his beard,
The pain well hidden
Beneath his grin.
Then like that child
Of long ago
He salutes the flag
America, U.S.A. ❀

While he eats
Cold monkeys' paws
Fed through cages
Of bamboo poles,

THE SONG

He hears somewhere
(or is it delusion?)
The voice of his child
Singing low.

He walks till sundown
His broken back numbed
Bamboo ends stuck in his thumbs.
He feels the flesh
Torn off his feet
Drape over rocks
As he stumbles on.
Convulsed with pain
He hears again
The singing voice
Of his waiting child.

He walks, he eats
He lives
Because somewhere (or is it delusion?)
He hears a voice
Singing low
Sweet Chariot. ✳

I've taught you how
To lay a splint
On broken sparrow wings.

I've brought home leaves
From mulberry trees
To feed your bottled friends.

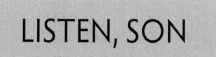

LISTEN, SON

I've sat you down
To make you see

How butterflies live free.

Today, my son
Let's talk about
How man lives to be free.

It takes the hand
That laid those splints,
It takes that heart
That brought home leaves,
It takes that dream
That unscrewed jars,
It takes all three
To make man live.

It takes a man
To make man free. ✤

DADDY

You taught me how
To lay a splint
On broken sparrow wings.

You brought home leaves
From mulberry trees
To feed my crawly friends.

You sat me down
To make me see
How butterflies live free.

Today I saw you take your gun,
Hunter's license and your boots,
I saw you leave as the sun
Gently touched my sparrow wings. ✳

VOICE TO THE FLAG

The rainbow you cast below God's own
Was not by one voiced Let There Be You.
It was mine, my umbilical cord
Twisted and coiled who damned the flow
Of hemorrhaging rivers, passion on ice
So you may live above us all.

The red of your beat was not by His voice
Nor the blue, the white of your eyes.
It was this hand which bears the cross
Of that creation currents ago
Who met each throe from wintry skies
So you may live, the mother of all. ✹

The wooden soldier marches
As he was wound to do.
Steadily, rhythmically,
Mechanical precision.

The only dislocation
Between manufactured knees.
The wooden soldier marches
Then stands perfectly still,
A soldier no more
But a wooden peg.

But the soldier I know
Keeps on marching.

THE WOODEN SOLDIER

He keeps on beating
For he has no key
To stop him from seeing
Dislocated limbs
Of children on children.
He has no key
To stop him from smelling
The river of blood
On Sunday afternoons.

Forgive us, O Soldier
For factorizing keys
Only for soldiers
On wooden knees.
Forgive us, soldier
For mechanized birds,
Wooden logs and battlefields. ✿

Howard Johnson
Enter
Toll gate
Next Service Area

HELLO WORLD

7 miles
Blinkers
Accelerator
Rearview mirror
Speed—
45 miles

70 miles
Next Exit
5 miles
Food
Lodging
Lights
Calif.
Conn.
Mich.
Last Service Area
Exhaustion
Exit
Howard Johnson.

The only communication with the world
As one travels past each exhaust pipe
The man-made art of mountainous billboards
And prisoned license plates
Along the speedway of
Turnpike, USA. ✼

SUNDAY AFTERNOON

Silence grows louder,
Raindrops fall longer.
Clouds drop lower,
Winds sing gentler.
Rooms feel emptier,
The heart aches deeper.
Petals look softer,
The grass stands colder.
Steps walk slower
The sun sets longer.
It's Sunday
In the afternoon. ✸

Stall number 7
To shift to park.
Press button up
To door 207.

APARTMENT 207

P.O. Box given
To keep me from straying,
Telephone number on page 111.

I live these numbers
Printed by man.

Carry the key
To match 207.
I ought to know
What, Where and Why,
My keys all fit
Except for one lie.
My pulses beat
Not in 7s
My dreams are not numbered,
Not 7, 11.
I park and live 207
But my heart still cries
Hell or Heaven
Where am I going?
Where do I belong? ✳

FOR RENT

Why can't man
Be fully furnished
Like apartments advertised
In today's ads?

How can I gamble
Down payment on man
Whose soul echoes hollow
The silence of each room
The curtainless windows
Of his concrete walls,

And the lemon-waxed blocks
Of his linoleum heart?

Take me to the hills
Instead. ✷

THE GOLDEN HOUR

The flower picker
Picks
Orchids off each
Golden spike.
Burned and singed
He toils till night
Blind to nature's
Radiant blush.
He feels the strike
Of each golden ray
Hot and hard
Upon his back.
From dawn to dusk
He swears and picks
Numb to all but the rage
Of each golden hour
Of minimum wage. ✺

A LESSON

In my youth
I held no keys
But living
Has taught me
Good.

ON MAKING A GLASS OF LEMONADE, FROM THE POINT OF VIEW OF A LEMON

I burst and flow
To his beat I grow.
He squeezes me dry
No tears to cry.
He stirs me to taste
To his dying thirst.
He feeds my seeds
To his stainless throat.
I satiate needs
Once man I fed.
Now juiceless I lay
Like sunbaked clay
Useless and smashed
At the bottom of trash. ✳

THE SPECTATOR

In the burial grounds of senses lay
One man alone who thinks he lives.

He quenches thirst with scotch and water.
He watches bathers in the sea.

He sits in joy as two lovers
Love on cinema screen and TV.

Unlike the frog who plunges in
Off his pad of native green,

Unlike the child who hunts and finds
That cherry in the forgotten fields,

He eats the fruits of Sara Lee
Thawed and warmed at 300 degrees.

He presses play to hear the rape
Of nature's song on plastic tape.

Herein lives a man
Dead. ✺

ARTICHOKE

Did it grow
Layer on layer
Leaf upon leaf
Only for this?

With two fingers he took the first,
Hanging loose from the base.
He dipped it twice in hollandaise sauce,
Raked it once through his teeth.
He took what little was offered him
On the tip of that leaf green.
Then dropped it carelessly
Into a bowl.
Around the base he took it by number,
One by one, as with the first.
He ran each skin between his teeth
Until he came to a tighter fist.
He found the petals too soft to take
The mark of his teeth, the pick of his hand.
He scooped the petals, laid them aside,
He took his knife to scrape it clean.
Sliced it in fourths to fit his bite,
He stabbed each part for the rite,
Consummation of the heart. ✸

A GRAIN OF SAND

How can you know
The magnificence
Of a grain of sand
Except to have it
In your eyes
Or to feel it crushed
Between your teeth
Hidden in cuisine
Of hot buttered clams? ✺

A man and his woman quietly sit,
Her grey in a bun, his hair in a bald.
They show no bond except for a ring
Proclaiming vows between the two.

OVERCOOKED PEAS FROM EYES OF THE YOUNG

They use their eyes on
overcooked peas,
They touch their legs
against Lysoled chairs.
Their lips only move
to meet each spoon
They sit and eat, a
man and his woman.

Damn you, woman,
How can you sit
Concentrating on peas?
How can you not share
Your thoughts over his?
How can you not feel
His pulses beat?
How can you waste
The presence of him?

Damn you, woman, look at his eyes,
Damn you, man, don't look at your peas.
Tell her your sighs, your woes, your dreams,
How can you sit and look at your peas?
Where is that touch, that look, that feel
That once had formed that golden ring?

Damn you both, for dying so young.
Damn you both, for looking at peas. ✱

THEY

Dearly beloved
In holy matrimony
You are joined
As one: husband and wife.

He

He returns home daily
Climbing staircases
Rejecting elevators
In-between spaces.

He looks at candles
As scentless saviors
For darkened nights
When lightning strikes.

He prefers the flesh
Of artichoke hearts
Bottled and pickled
By S & W.

He bends over shelves
For *Newsweek, Time*
Popular Mechanics
National Geographic.

Ah, yes,
Dearly Beloved
Husband for wife.

She

She lives the risks
Of broken shafts
Hums a tune to elevator buzz.
Emergency buttons are just a fuss.

She fills the walls
With scented shadows
Winter, Spring, even Summer
Candles glow to golden slumber.

She seeks them fresh
From market trays
Not for the heart but for the joy
Of undressing leaves for
        artichoke hearts

She feels the chills
Along her spine
Between the leaves
Of Browning, Blake.
She presses flowers

Between the lines
Current facts
Of *Newsweek, Time.*

Ah, yes
Dearly Beloved
Husband and wife. ❀

TWO FOR THE ROAD ON SCOTCH AND WATER

He laid it down close
On a napkin to hold its moist.

Like a stream she sees it begin,
The little droplets, forming, joining,
Dripping, wetting until absorbed
By the sheet on which it waits.
She touches her fingers to the moist,
Slowly runs her fingers down.
The wet continues into her hand,
Slipping though her fingers
Warmed by her touch.

She takes it in her dripping hand,
Draws it up to her waiting lips,
Bottoms Up! And Dry!
She returns the glass
To moistened sheets
She snaps her fingers to the man.
Another scotch and water, please! ✾

LOVE

Through chrysalis jade
I watched it grow
Then set it free
So it could live.

How many wings
How many flights
Before it can be freed
Without a tear
Without a cry? ✽

BUBBLE

Spasmodic with sunlight
Psychedelic and high
Busting free
To its splattering end.

I longed to hold it
To make it mine.
But it was gone
With just a touch.

Crescenting above
Two heavenly bodies
Interlocked
On mortal grounds. ✺

IT

It enters and exits
Without being seen,
Bypassing hostesses
Too busy to free
Eyes from glitter,
Plastic trim.

Catch it now
Before it's gone.

Hold it close
Hold it fast.

Make it yours
Before it's gone,

Catch it now! ✳

ON SALE

I walk the city under neon lights
Watching shoppers dodge and fight
The endless maze of traffic rush.

They toss pennies
In corner pails
As chimes ring out
All joy to the world.
They hang out wreaths
On windowpanes
They wrap and curl
Green plastic bows.
They've listened good
To the Adman's soul.
He's promised them Joy,
Peace and Love,
Happiness, Goodwill,
Hallelujah to all.

I wonder how many people here tonight
Fear the coming of the promised morn. ✻

LONELINESS

The distances spread
Into a million miles
As the rooms of my soul
Swept clean of hope
Echo the beats
Of an empty pail. ❋

I'LL BLOW OUT THE CANDLE TOMORROW

Stay, I cry.
But he stands
And walks away
"It's time to go." ❋

Selected Poems from

THE PATH OF
BUTTERFLIES

RUN, RUN, BUT NOT INTO THE FOG

A little boy
Runs into the fog
As it slowly creeps
Over the field,
Softening edges
Into mists.
He runs and runs
And soon is swallowed
By the mysterious giant.
Then slowly, quietly
He returns to me
With wooden legs
And puddled wings.
"The more I ran
the more it disappeared." ✸

DON'T JUST TWINKLE, LITTLE STAR

The first bright star
Of the evening skies,
How many wishes
Do you prescribe?
Tell me, star
What have you done
With all those wishes
I've sent each night? ❀

WHY I TWINKLE, LITTLE ONE

Had I sent
Your first to you,
You would have stopped
Looking for me.
And what wonders
You would have missed,
Keeping your eyes
Away from me. ✽

RAGGEDY ANN

Stay.

Someday soon
Your handmade look
Of crescent smile
And crimson shag
Will be held
By every child,
As they caress
Cottoned arms
And buttoned eyes.

Someday soon,
When plastic hugs
And crustacean limbs
All become one
With our own,
As we confuse
Chemic tears
With our own...
Someday soon.

Wait. ✿

No wine, no candlelight,
But the kiss of the sun.
A toast to the bloom
Of a marigold.

CELEBRATION OF A MARIGOLD

Velvet red roses
And Queen Anne's lace
Carefully curtsy
From sterilized places.
While in the corner
Of a concrete porch,
Empty Coke bottles
And half an ashtray,
Paralyzed mops and straw-tied brooms,
The blooming of a marigold.

Sun-baked petals
Of custard-brown hues
Openly meet the golden sun,
As the voice they behold
Shouts aloud,
"I am born! I am born!"

No wine, no candlelight,
Only the kiss of the sun
Rejoice the blooming
Of a marigold. ❀

The long black serpent
Coils and waits
In ginger blossoms
And bamboo groves.

ROAD TO HANA, MAUI

Concealed by
Fragrance
And waterfalls
She lies in wait
For one little
Traveler
Down her back
Of sensuous scheme
Of curvatures.
Soon a traveler
Entranced
By fragrance,
Waterfalls,
And luscious bearings,
Clings on her back
And travels deep—
Into the wonders
Of her path,
And knows not when
Her wretched venom
Becomes his own,
As he retches
And spits
From his gut
Into a bed
Of heliconia blood. ✳

SPIDER

He spreads untouched
Between two branches.
His absolute freedom,
A phenomenal wonder
Until one nears
The intricate threads
Nakedly spun
From spider to branches. ✽

ROOTS

A flower cut
From rooted ground
Quickly yields
To human hands. ✽

RED HIBISCUS

She blooms, then clings
Till shriveled veins
Slowly burn
Her clutching hands. ✽

UNTITLED

In the middle of a forest
A great big branch
Brushes across the sky. ✿

BAMBOO

Like a man,
It reaches out.
The higher it grows,
The lower it stoops. ✿

UNTITLED

After the rainfall
A little white butterfly
Lightly soars. ❀

She sneaks into the night,
Pin picks doors.
She blows out candles,
Eliminates dreams.

She ruffles feathers,
Stores away pillows.
She turns ignitions
In parking garages.
She overturns cans,
And cancels mirages.

DAWN

She steps on tails
Jackhammer rails,
She presses ON
Until the breath
That calmly hummed
Yells and screams
To be heard.

Good Morning!

From a Lover...To Dawn
    Stay away.

Leave me one morningless night
Where silence speaks the only vows.

Lingering kisses,
Silent touches.
Gathering pulses,
Paradise avowed.
Stay away.   Thief. ✳

THE UNLIBERATED

If I were a woman
Married to a man
Who brought me a rose
For no reason at all—

I'd scrub his floors
And wash his socks.
I'd dust his clubs
And fishing rods
I'd buy him *Playboy*
And Pouilly-Fuissé.
I'd scrub his back
And never refuse.
If he brought me a rose
For no reason at all. ❀

THE LIBERATED

A rose is a rose
Even to one
Who bears the name
Of husband or other.

If she gave me a rose
For no reason at all,
I'd rub her neck
And scrub the floor.
I'd starch the sheets
And feed the cat.
I'd leave the house
To give her an hour
To paint or write
Her poetic calls.
If she gave me a rose
For no reason at all. ✿

TO A PEN

Quilled and feathered
You left a right
To swords or song
For our fathered child.

The song is dead
The swordsmen claim,
And blindly take
The victor's stance.
But somewhere still
In the closing night
A newborn child
Clearly hears
The melody
Of your promised song. ✾

VIEW FROM A HOSPITAL BED

A branch outside
My window pane
Gently moves only by breeze.
It sways in limbo,
Not touching the sill
Or the roof below.
Then slowly comes
To a gentle still
As the sun
Slowly
Sinks
Into
The
Night. ✴

ON THE EVE OF SURGERY

An unfriendly morn
Awaits my awakening.
Whatever his face
I'll greet him with mine.
If his breath
Should suck mine dry.
I'll take his hand
Into mine,
And gently leave
By morning's light. ✵

In total chaos
A thousand-piece spread
Overturned, strewn, piece upon piece
Reds, violets, white against black
Senseless, meaningless
No magical code to make them whole
Except for the fitting of piece into piece.

JIGSAW PUZZLE

The formation of the border,
 the first glimmer of hope
Four quartered corners,
 strategically placed
While in the center
A mountainous mass

Saved for the coming
Of the final score.

Fingers searching, pushing, forcing
Piece into piece for a whole among parts.
The edges sharp into the smooth,
The curvatures small for a clutching fit.
The turning, twisting, tossing trials
For one sudden fit of a connecting cry.
Sometimes a fit irrationally found
Just by staring
At one little piece.

Edge against edge, mounts into shape;
Piece into piece, the center grows
From border to mass, a disappearing space,
The external shine bruised by handling.
A final whole after the parts
By one little piece of insignificant form
Snugly pushed for the resurrected whole. ✖

DEAR JOHN

I
Don't
Love
You
Any
More.

From six separate pages
Of *Webster's Third*,
A death more brutal
Than iron and steel. ✳

I envy the geese
As they spread their wings,
Voicing their flight
In capital V.

FROM A SPARROW

What special gift
Schedules their lives
Without an error
Every winter, every spring?

Whose callous hand
Bypassed this nest?
I keep on falling
As I spread my wings.
No course to fly
Except by chance.

Do geese in flight
Ever fall?
Take to flight
In summer skies?

Why was the sparrow
Denied the gift
Of scheduled flights
And course to fly? ❀

"Other people,"
"Other men,"
"They," and "someone"
And "everyone else."
How very simple
To become "them."
But my voice
Will not allow
Such migration
Of my soul. ✾

THE FORGOTTEN WORLD

They rock and wait.
They rock and wait.

The world's a mirror
Wherever he turns.
He sees his face
On every face.
Toothless, neutral,
Frozen into space.
His dignity hidden
In arthritic veins.
His only hope
At swinging doors
For a voice
Calling Dad.
But the only voice
Comes in shifts—
Starched, immaculate,
Antiseptically clean.
And soon that glint
Lays at rest
As he rocks and nods
In silent wait. ✵

TO THE YOUNG

These hearts which seem
To outlive us all
Once soared with passion
Like your own.
And now we sit
In silent wait
Tasting salt
From long ago
Beaches. ✤

REFLECTIONS FROM A WHEELCHAIR ON VISITING DAY

The clocks have stolen
Those unicorn days,
But dreams and hopes
Have no ages.
So we sit and wait
In silent walls
For phoenixes
Out of ashes. ✹

GIFTS UNACKNOWLEDGED

Somewhere a child
Catches a star,
Whispers a wish
As the moon
Softly smiles
Over her head.
Somewhere still,
A woman peers
Through curtainless glass,
Toothlessly smiles
And thanks Above
For another night,
Another light.

While over the Mohave
The moon awaits
In patient silence,
And the desert sleeps,
Undisturbed.
A million stars
Above the sleep
No child, no woman
No one to touch.
The desert sleeps... ❀

ONLY A NAME

Last night a man
Leaped to a heap
Right below my apartment wall.

The ambulance, the police,
Flash cubes and reporters,
Curious bystanders, all in droves
For a name and an address
And who saw him last.

The whispering, the silence, the sudden shock—
Who was he? Why did he jump?
The bloody puddle below my window
Of someone's son, someone's friend.
Now a number on statistic's wall.

An hour and soon
The caking of the puddle
Around its edges toward the deep.
The growing murmurs, a giggle, a laugh,
Even a kiss exchanged by two—
Who was he? Why did he jump?
Only a man who couldn't make it,
That seems all.

Except for the red in the concrete walk,
A vacant parking lot once again,
As each returns to his own little room.
And nothing else.

A voice in the dark, a young man's grief
Calling into the night.
Come back. Bernie, come back.
A hopeless sob and nothing else.

Who was he? Why did he jump?
Did I once share a ride going up or maybe down?
Did I once step aside as he took his laundry down?
Had I smiled, would he have known
He was not alone at all? ✿

THE CLOWN

From the corner
Of his eye
A little teardrop
Seeks a path
Down his cheek
And leaves not a smear
On his painted smile. ✳

AFTER LIFE

Lichened with scales,
A tombstone leans
While through its crack
A morning glory twines,
Covering
A
Chiseled
Name. ✻

CHERRY BLOSSOM

Radiantly soft
She enters on stage.
She sings one song
Then exits on.
Her song fills each
With joyous pain
As the lights turn on
An empty stage. ✹

Section V

Dangerous and Ageless

A forty-year-old man choked with tears when he read "Sundays at 5 P.M." (See page 200.) "You really know all about Sunday afternoons," he said.

A ninety-year-old woman nodded and thanked me for "Ginsberg's Burlap Bag." (See page 183.) "Yes," she said, "that passion never ages even if our bodies do."

"Can I have your phone number when you become 88?" requested an elderly man playfully after hearing my poem "When I Am 88." (See page 182.)

They have confirmed that this thing called life, with all its passion, feelings and sexuality, belongs to us—men and women of all ages.

We still see things we shouldn't see —
We still feel things we shouldn't feel —
We still hear things we shouldn't hear —
We still taste grief, joy, fear.
In a world that vibrates
Through all of my senses.
We are not dead yet. ✤

I will have a love affair
That will leave me
Trembling
On a windless day.

WHEN I AM 88

I will drown in Puccini,
Mozart, Verdi...
Tidal waves roaring
Inside of me.

I will feel the brush strokes
Of van Gogh,
Clawing, blinding
Driving me mad.

I will do Shakespeare,
Vibrant on stage,
Rivers rushing, splashing
Over moss and stone.

I will become soft,
Sensuous, wet
Against your skin,
Silk against steel.

When I am 88
I will be woman,
Yes! I will still be woman. ✹

GINSBERG'S BURLAP BAG

I want to make love
With Ginsberg's
Burlap bag.
I want to feel
The coarseness
Of the weaves
Against my skin.
I want to suck
Juices out of every thread,
Feel it dribble...down
My breasts.
I want to find words
To shrivel in my mouth,
Taste every word,
Dried leaves embossed
With drawings
Of strangers' faces
Like death. ✸

Images, illusions,
Recklessly formed,
Invade her.

Conversations
Unmatched by any
Pulitzer dialogue
Fluids through her head.

Feelings bruised
Around the edges
Ache for undefined elsewheres
And ocean waves.

Little stirrings
In the gut
Turn into
Unwritten poems.

Protected
By private existence,
She becomes
(in her own image)
A mysterious,
Desirous woman
Stimulated
(illusions! illusions!)
Merely because
A stranger gave her a glance. ✳

A RELATIONSHIP, UNNAMED

Language would ruin
My relationship.
Best left to silence.
Best left unsaid, explored
By that part of me
That offers no words.
Undefined, unrecognized,
Left buried somewhere
Slightly between the lines. ✸

HI, MY NAME IS FRANCES

I sent you a puzzle
Without the pieces.
Only my name
On the box.

Then, like a game,
I email the pieces,
One by one,
Day by day.

You take pieces
Shove them to fit,
Shout back others,
"It doesn't fit!"

Ah, love, don't you know,
All the hours, all the days
Won't be time enough
To fit the pieces
Into my frame. ❊

GEORGIA O'KEEFFE'S CALENDAR

Your brush strokes
    Alluring
        Caressing
            Quivering...

How many men, Georgia,
Did you suck in with your art?

    Two calla lilies on Pink
    Purple Petunias
    Oriental Poppies,
    Red Canna
    Blue Morning Glories

We were the models.
We let you use us shamelessly.
We turned to the light, opened our petals
To the pink of our secret places.
We let you see what you already knew.
They, they knew nothing.

Bravo, Georgia. ✺

TO WOMEN OF PASSION

Sylvia, Sara, Virginia,
Why.
Why did you
Snuff out the fires
That burned so fiercely
In you?

Were you afraid
This passion that savaged you
On both ends
Would burn itself out?

Were you so afraid
This passion would die on you,
And you could not live
Life without fire?
You could not live it with?

Fools. ✺

"Black is for old people.
Brown is for old people."
Her birthday has escalated to 80.
"I'm going to go backwards from now on,"

BLACK IS FOR OLD PEOPLE

She tells her grandson. "I'll be 79 next year."

"When I'm old," she tells me,
"I'm not going to those places
To crochet, play bingo, sew bottle caps to make hotplates.
That's for old people.

"When I'm old, I'm going to live near a movie theater
So I can see movies instead of being with old people."
At age 85, on my calendar, her voice echoes:
"I must be getting old."

After Alzheimer's muted her voice
I took her script and added to her wardrobe,
Lavender, light blue, green dusters, elasticized pull-up pants,
Loose blouses for easy access for stiffened arms.

Nothing in brown or black.
Black and brown are for old people.

"Bring in a blouse for the final viewing of her body at the wake"
Sinks into the new reality.

A rush to the mall... the chilled January winds whipping through
    my hair...

She needs to be warm... She needs to be warm...
Black is for old people. Brown is for old people.

I move hangers in petite size for a lavender or a blue woolen coat...
Where in Hawaii will I find a lavender woolen coat?
Spent from my search, with hands on the clock racing away...
I settle for the only petite-sized coat, in brown.
Okasan, I'm sorry, I'm sorry, I know brown is for old people.
But this will keep you warm on your final journey.

I add a tiara on her head,
Sprinkle Vanda orchids over her folded hands.
I hear a chuckle. ✹

PASSION

Red

ink

drips

from

the

tip

of

her

pen

Long after her last written word. ✾

THE HUMAN BUFFET

They come to me
Like starving beasts
Gorging, gorging
On whatever meets
Their hungry need
Stuffing themselves
With gluttony.
The vultures at least
Will wait 'til I'm dead. ✦

ERASABLE PENCIL #2

Crossword puzzles, first draft memos,
Notes to the teacher, grocery shopping lists.
Telephone messages, long additions,
Essay exams, dentist dates.
All done
In erasable #2.

Tell me true,
Your penciled note
In this Valentine? ✳

A ROSE FROM A FRIEND

the
fragrance
of the rose
delicate as
lattice work
designed
by its rose bugs. ✿

I am generations of women
Looking in at layers of silk kimonos,
Muffled giggles, *koto** movement,
Knowing they can only be
Mere images of desire.

NISEI* WOMAN

I am generations of women
Waiting to be dragonfly wings,
A maple leaf, spiraling snowflake,
A cherry blossom,
Released and detached from
Generations of cultural clasps.

I am generations of women,
Suppressed in thin *yukata***
Stuck ankle deep in rice fields,
Scarecrows on wooden stakes.
Denied, yet desiring wantonness
Beneath layers of silk.

I am woman,
Invisible.
Dying. ✽

*Nisei: Second-generation Japanese; *Koto*: a traditional Japanese stringed
musical instrument; *Yukata*: cotton kimono

BECOMING SANSEI*

My fingers bleed
From untying obi knots.
Layer after layer of kimono silk
Free to flow, clinging
Wet against my skin.

Won't the sun rise?

Slowly, so slowly, I unwrap myself
And gently fall
Silk clouds at my feet.
Standing naked, becoming.

I kneel to lift cherry blossoms,
A chrysanthemum,
The aroma of green tea
Under global skies.

I become obi knots,
Untied. ✸

*Sansei: Third-generation Japanese-American

SILK AND STEEL

Ah yes,
Silk and steel.

Silk...
    Delicate as butterfly wings,
    Against my skin,
    Soft, fragile seeming,
    Yet, wound beyond tears—
    My ancestral birth.

Steel...
    Beneath layers of woven silk
    On the slopes of Fuji and Mauna Kea,
    Bamboo groves clothing
    One generation
    Into the next.

Silk and Steel.
Ribbons of my inner Samurai. ✽

UNTITLED

I walk faceless
in the crowd
faceless...
until found
by you. ✳

THE HUNTER

The tigress prowls
Through the forests,
Feeling the moist
Of the morning dew
Against her velvet thighs.
She moves, aware
Of the hunter in her midst.

The hunter narrows his aim,
Yet is unable to shoot
The tigress pauses in his crosshairs
Denying him
The hunter's game. ✻

It is that time,
Whether clocked at Pacific, Eastern
Or Greenwich Mean,
For that relentless ache •

SUNDAYS AT 5 P.M.

To slowly overtake Sunday afternoons,
An ache that has no name,
Just an ache of emptiness,
Unfulfilled dreams and
Unlived moments yet to come.

It is a time for healing...
A time to smooth jagged edges
Of shattered crystals crunching
Under naked feet.
A time to tweeze each splinter of pain
From the young and the aged.

It is a time for forgiving...
A time to unlatch doors
Of the caged,
So each can soar to its destination
With messages of peace.

It is a time for solitude,
La Bohème, the blues
Spoken silences.
It is, above everything else,
A hell of a time
For a woman
Not born for
Sunday afternoons. ✹

AT THE END OF A MOVING DAY

I have packed and scrubbed
Room by room, closet by closet,
For the movers
This immaculate house,
Sadness instead of content.
The city lights
High against Diamond Head
Conceal lives not my own.
I want to be elsewhere
Among poets, unicorns—
Pagliacci clowns,
Sparrows, snowflakes,
Magnolia blossoms.

From an empty room
A television set shouts
Images by someone else.
I don't want his images.
I want my own.

I want my own. ✸

Transformation...
A new moon hangs in darkness,
A lady in waiting.

DOUBLE TRANSFORMATION

Two strangers, unknown
Except by name
Meet beneath the promise of moon.

First slice of light,
A crescent in the skies
Smiling things to come.

Transformation continues
The gentle probing
To see what is and what is not.

A half moon...
Dances metamorphosis,
Near perfection.

Soon caution ventures
Into places without permission,
Poems late at night.

The full moon...
A circle of creation.
Her journey's end.

Trespasses beyond the moon,
A joyous ache
Softening edges... ✸

THE BUGLER

Life would be quite bearable
With no sunsets,
Evening dusk, sparrows
Returning home.
(Their last song), a bugler's call.
Life would be quite bearable
Without dusk,
Reflections, introspection,
Ardent dreams, undefined wishes,
Were one not born a Pisces,
Whose restless soul, paralleled,
With opposing face
Wandering, wandering
Without sunsets,
Following,
Poemless. ❀

how utterly boring
to have a partner
of perfection

how utterly utterly lucky
to have a friend
just like me

A NON-PUNCTUATED PARTNER

it's my silent voice
blind spots and
spaces
that bring life
to the dead

white-crested waves against
shoreline rocks
glass topped ponds
in still of winter

how utterly utterly lucky
to know someone
who can't be read like
a novel beginning to end

a partner without periods
commas dashes apostrophes
exclamations parentheses
a partner covered with ellipses...

how very very lucky
to have a friend
of such imperfection ✸

I search out the window
For the sound of Mozart.
My fingers freeze on the keyboard
At what I see.

MOZART PLAYED TWICE

He is on hard concrete,
Labors away under the hot summer sun,
His strands of long hair stuck to his face,
His t-shirt, wet against his skin,
Faded denims, rolled twice over,
A trough for sawdust and dirt.
The buzz of his electric saw, staccato pounding,
Hammer against nails
The Mozart blasting from a radio.
His voice in vibrato.

Another vision comes into play:
Mozart vibrates concert halls.
Hammer pounding,
Baton waving,
Hammer waving,
Baton pounding.
Men in penguin suits accompanied
By the finery drenched in deep perfume.
Mozart, without vibrato.

Mozart in two concert halls
Outside my window. ❀

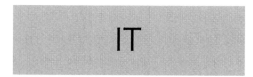

IT

Emily Dickinson never saw it
But she was certain of it.
She ached for it
In her attic.

Elizabeth Browning
Counted it
In her sonnets
From the Portuguese.

Abelard and Heloise
Mythicized it.
Impressionists painted it.
Hepburn screened it.

If you wish to know
How it can be yours,
Become
A dangerous woman. ✤

OLD MAN

An old man of the sea sits
Watching two young lovers
Murmuring *enpassant*
Ah yes, ah yes. ✽

SUICIDE

He snuffed out his own candle

Left us all in darkness. ✽

SOME MEN

Some men get up at night,
Stare at lights in silent rage,
The city lights blink their digital faces
Stealing heartbeats, cornered in cages.

Some men get up at night,
Cry out in terror, a bottle in hand,
Flat and dead, flat and dead,
While neon blinks, too late, too late.

Some men get up at night,
Stare at ceilings with peeling paint,
Faint traces of girls they've never kissed,
Sports cars they've never raced.

Some men get up at night
Living in the wake of was.
Love lost was never theirs.
They had their time,
They had their time. ✾

STRAYERS

Some
        men
                should

        not
    be
            allowed
                    to
                        stray
                            into
                                our
                                    lives,
those
        who
            cannot

        stay... ✳

Every night like clockwork,
A loud pounding on the wooden door.
He stands there, a shadow in jacket and boots,
Bearing armloads of firewood.

MY
GATEKEEPER

His smile extends from his eyes
To his mouth through a grey
    moustache.
He walks in, unloads the firewood
With a dull thud.
Muchas gracias, Señor.

He is a burro laden down
With lichened twigs and branches,
Unloads the burden from his back,
His smile, richer than hot chocolate.
Every night he unties his thick rope
And log by log, fills the hearth,
Nods his service in silence.
Si. Si. Muchas gracias.

Who are you, Don Jose?
So humble, so silent.
You don't speak English,
What do you speak?
Do you seduce women with lines from Neruda?
Do you captivate them with tales from Borges?
Could you be my Don Juan,
Laughing at my 'gracias.'
Could you make love in English
Or in Spanish, burning
My fantasies into red hot ashes? ✹

WATER

on my back, naked
I was born.
the first drop of rain chills
where the first severance began,
     between my legs.
        a stream
           trickles where life began anew
              the first cold bite turns warm.

soon, another awakening:
like a child's crayoned sun,
     its center, another river
        running over my stomach,
          running down the hill,
            through the meadows
              rolling trembles
                through my body.

my heartbeat waits
after the short,
   fast,
      passing
        rain. ✽

We are the dangerous women...
Who never say no to sunsets, sunrises,
Evening strolls or double martinis.

DANGEROUS WOMEN

We are the women who speak to you
In supermarkets over apples and cabbages.
Making you wish you could follow us home.

We are the women taught by mothers
To make you feel we could be yours
No matter who you are.

We are the women who extract
Extraordinary days out of the ordinary,
Leaving ache and joy in empty spaces.

We are the women who write poems,
Send you copies without permission,
Capture moonbeams in your name.

We are the gatherers of dreams,
Fantasizing scenes
In private places where your secrets live.

We are not easy to be with
After sad movies, romantic novels,
Or on Sunday afternoons.

We are so damn demanding
You wish we had never met,
Yet you know, we are the only poetry you have.

Yes, we are the dangerous women: vulnerable,
Ageless, poetic, passionate, life with two feet
Slightly off the ground.

We are the women you should avoid
If you don't believe in Peter Pan,
And the first star of the evening skies.

But pour us wine as the sun sets low,
And we will hand you the key
To things you don't know. ✹

DEFINITION

Do not define me by age.
I am not Roosevelt, Truman,
Eisenhower, or JFK.

Do not define me by blue veins
bulging out on my spidery arms,
my gobbler, once a Hepburn, Audrey.

Do not define me by Rorschach,
On skin brushed with indelible ink.
A Pollock on the wall of MOMA.

Do not define me by a new dance step
Shuffling, shuffling—
My heels replaced by clogs.

I am
a rabbit out of a hat,
a three-ring circus without net,
A whodunit without clues.
War and Peace, chapter one,
The second act.

I am
Without epilogue. ✺

Acknowledgments

Will someone find me the words to thank the following:

To all the men and women who strayed into my life and couldn't stay, and to those who stayed, you all were and are a rich source of poetry.

To Linda Donahue, my first editor, for her gentle edits, even after I asked her to be brutal.

To Nicole Antonio who generously typed the poems from my four earlier published books.

To poet Red Slider for sending me back to the drawing board with his "This is a good outline, now fill in the spaces," or "Now get rid of the clichés." Thank you for the hours spent on my poetry even if I went on hours not speaking to you because you didn't say my drafts were masterpieces.

To George Engebretson, Duane Kurisu and Dawn Sakamoto of Watermark Publishing for giving me life as a poet. Dawn, your knowledge, expertise and guiding hand are beyond description.

To artist Jason Kimura, who knew even before he saw the manuscript, the colors for the book cover. Thank you for the dangerous art work.

And to all the published writers and poets who give me inspiration with your work, beginning with that poet who wrote about flowers nodding their heads in the wind.

– FHK

Index of Poems

About the Author

The award-winning, internationally published author of fourteen books, and a regular column, "Dear Frances," for caregivers in the *Hawai'i Herald*, Frances H. Kakugawa conducts poetry readings, workshops and lectures throughout the country. In her sessions for adults, Frances shares with honesty and openness the lessons learned from caregiving. Programs for hospital and elder-healthcare professionals focus on humanizing their clinical skills. In her children's workshops, Frances introduces students to poetry as a way to explore and embrace their elders and other aspects of their lives.

Frances presently resides in Sacramento, Calif., and leads a monthly poetry support group for the caregivers for the Alzheimer's Association and a Memoir Miners writing group at the Asian Community Center.

To book Frances for a workshop, classroom visit or lecture, email her at fhk@francesk.org or contact her online on her Facebook Page (www.facebook.com/FrancesKakugawa) or on her blog (franceskakugawa.wordpress.com).

✺

53648037R10123

Made in the USA
San Bernardino, CA
24 September 2017